Psychological Wisdom

In A Nutshell

By Psychologist

"Dr. Dan" Matzke, PhD

A Collection Of
Uplifting Thoughts, Ideas & Perspectives
For Personal Development
Peak Performance & Well-Being

For information about other books and programs by Dr. Dan visit: *DrDanMatzkePhD.com*

About "Dr. Dan"

Dan Matzke, a.k.a. "Dr. Dan", holds a Ph.D. in psychology. Dr. Dan worked as a licensed Psychologist and Marriage & Family Therapist for over 25 years. He taught psychology classes and did consulting work (testing & evaluations), prior to retiring from private practice in California and moving to Jackson Hole, Wyoming. He now enjoys writing and mentoring, when not hiking, fishing, skiing, traveling or flying. Dr. Dan has a commercial pilot's license, with flight instructor ratings for airplanes and gliders. He is a winner of the highly prized Barron Hilton Soaring Cup.

Dedication Note:

To my wife and life partner – Julie. Thanks for all of your support. It has been a *grand adventure...*

Acknowledgements:

Insights and ideas for this book were drawn from many contemporary writers, who have in turn drawn from seminal thinkers and authors throughout history. Interested readers are referred to the books of Aaron T. Beck, Albert Ellis, Viktor Frankl, Abraham Maslow, Rollo May, Carl Rogers, Robert C. Solomon and Irvin D. Yalom.

Disclaimer:

The information provided in this book is informative and educational in nature and is NOT intended as counseling, therapy, psychological treatment and/or psychiatric advice. If you are experiencing acute or chronic emotional problems or symptoms such as anxiety, depression, mood swings, suicidal thoughts, and/or severe symptoms such as auditory hallucinations (hearing voices) or visual hallucinations (seeing things that other people do not see), and/or are feeling overly suspicious or paranoid, and/or are having problems related to drugs or alcohol – it is strongly recommended that you contact a local counseling service, mental health center, psychiatric office and/or your personal medical doctor. Help and hope are available through these sources and you are encouraged to seek it as soon as possible!!

Preface:

This book is a multi-volume work of five previously published programs – including Success Over Personal Development Pitfalls, Success Over Stress & Burnout, Success Over Stinkin' Thinkin', Emotional Intelligence – Successful Personality, and Real-Life Intelligence – The Edge For Successful Living. It is a collection of powerful tools and skills for personal growth & development, peak performance and well-being – with uplifting thoughts, ideas and perspectives for success in life & living. The sections can be read individually as desired, or together as a collective series. The addendum contains three essence essays addressing the topics of Personal Effectiveness, Golden Guidelines for Life & Living and Mindfulness.

<u>Psychological Wisdom In A Nutshell</u>
A Five Volume Set

Success Over
Personal Development Pitfalls

By "Dr. Dan" Matzke, PhD

FAQ's Addressed In This Program:

Why is it so difficult to change
negative behaviors and attitudes?

What are the pitfalls to personal change,
growth and development?

How do payoffs, neurotic paradox and
euphoric recall play a role?

What are the keys for change and
success in personal development?

Table of Contents

Introduction - Pitfalls To Change

The questions arise - Why is it so difficult to change negative patterns of thinking and behavior? Why is it so tough to get out of self-defeating ruts, and to get free of toxic attitudes, myths and illusions? Three key factors can be identified - three pitfalls to change:

1. Payoffs

One of these pitfalls to change is the fact that there are payoffs. There are payoffs to negative thought patterns and self-defeating behaviors. For example, the Stinkin' Thinkin' of "Better Living Through Chemistry" has some very powerful and addictive payoffs. Through chemical means we can feel very good. We can eliminate a lot of tension, anxiety and pain – very quickly. There is a payoff for using chemistry.   If we're going to change this self-defeating behavior, if we're going to eliminate or modify this Stinkin' Thinkin', we're going to have to give up that payoff. Another example of payoff can be found in the "I'm OK (only) when I'm working" notion.   There are some real payoffs and benefits to working. We can earn money, we can achieve a certain standard of living, accumulate a lot of nice possessions. When you combine the attitude "More is Better" with "I'm OK when I'm working" (more work is better), you can accomplish a lot, achieve a lot, and have a lot of financial rewards. To get out of that rut, to change that self-defeating behavior, means that you might have to cut back on your standard of living.   You might have to settle for fewer or less extravagant material possessions.

One of the primary pitfalls to change is letting go of some of the payoffs, surrendering them - perhaps deciding that they cost too much or that the price is too high.

2. Neurotic Paradox

A second pitfall to change can be referred to as the neurotic paradox. The word neurotic refers to being overly anxious and irrational. The word paradox refers to something that is a contradiction, conflicting or inconsistent. Neurotic paradox describes the phenomenon that human beings, with all of our knowledge, understanding, information, and data about self-defeating behaviors, still engage in them and still do things that are toxic. For example, a person who's on a diet can have volumes of information about calories and nutrition, the importance of a balanced diet, and still find themselves at the refrigerator door, still reaching for that big piece of chocolate cake with ice cream on it. A person who is trying to beat a chemical dependency, who has information and knowledge about the chemical dependency process and addiction, may still find himself in a liquor store buying a six-pack of beer along with his cigarettes. He will still pop that beer, even though he knows that the first beer will open the door to a drinking or using spree. The paradox is - why do we do that? Even though we have that information, even though we have the understanding, the knowledge, why do we still engage in self-defeating behaviors?

The key seems to be in the time sequence, of what happens as we engage in these self-defeating behaviors. What our primal brain and body tends to remember is that through engaging in these behaviors, we can experience almost immediate relief. Our anxiety, our tension, our pain can be almost immediately taken away. We can start feeling good almost instantly. For example, on an empty stomach a couple sips of hard liquor will get you a warm glow in just a matter of minutes. All that tension and anxiety is just washed away. If you are snorting cocaine or amphetamines, it's just a matter of seconds after you inhale it that you get a rush, that good feeling, that euphoric sense. If you are injecting a drug such as heroine into your veins, it's instantaneous, as soon as you start the injection you get high. So relief is just a sip away, a swallow away, a snort away, or a shot away. That's what our inner brain remembers. That's what our body remembers.

Our intellect, our reason, has all that information and data about the negative side effects and negative consequences, but they do not happen at the same time. The suffering does not happen until later. You don't get the hangover until some time later, perhaps the next morning. You don't get the big bills from the compulsive shopping spree you went on until perhaps the end of the month when the charge cards come due. This time sequence is a key factor in the neurotic paradox. The primal brain and body remember that we can get almost immediate relief, satisfaction and pleasure, from engaging in many of these self-defeating behaviors. The negative side effects and consequences don't happen until some time later.

3. Euphoric Recall

A third pitfall to change, an element that makes it difficult to modify attitudes and behavior is a process called euphoric recall. This refers to the screening-out process of the mind when it tends to forget and selectively filter out the negative aspects and painful consequences of behavior. What we tend to remember are the positive things and the good times. An example could be if you went out drinking and partying with friends. The next morning you wake up and feel like you've been driven over by a truck — head pounding, throwing-up, etc. You might say, "I'm never going to do that again — it hurts too much." At the time you're quite serious and dedicated to that decision.

As time goes by, however, when you think back about that experience, what you'll tend to remember are the good times. You'll tend to remember how much fun you had out there partying with your friends and how good it felt at the time. What you'll tend to forget, what will fade, will be how bad you felt the next morning. The next time you're confronted with going out and practicing "better living through chemistry", what your primal mind is predominately going to remember, due to euphoric recall, is how good it felt. You'll tend to screen out or forget the negative aspects of the morning after.

In Summary – Three Pitfalls To Change:

1.)   The fact that toxic thinking and self-defeating behaviors often have strong payoffs, there are some appealing results that you would have to surrender and relinquish if you gave up the attitudes and behaviors.

2.) Neurotic paradox, the fact that relief is just a sip away, a swallow away, a snort away, a shot away. It's almost immediate.   You can feel good or get relief almost instantly – in spite of knowing better in the long run – because the negative consequences don't happen until some time later.

3.) Euphoric recall - a little trick that our mind plays on us as we recall past experiences - what we generally remember are the good times and how good it felt, and we tend to forget the negative side effects and consequences.

Keys To Lasting Change & Personal Development

So what are the keys to lasting change? What can one do to change toxic attitudes and self-defeating behaviors? Four key and critical steps can be identified:

1.   Awareness

The first step is to develop one's awareness and understanding of negative attitudes and actions and how they operate in one's life. Gaining this insight and perspective empowers a person to change. By reading and studying personal development programs (such as Dr.

Dan's programs on *Success Over Stress & Burnout* and *Success Over Stinkin' Thinkin'*), one can develop awareness and understanding of how toxic attitudes can affect one's actions.

2. Commitment

A second key step in changing toxic attitudes and self-defeating behaviors is to make a commitment - a direct decision to make a personal change. This has to be an individual choice, based on a realization that this doesn't work for me, the price is too high and it is costing me too much. It is not a choice that anyone else can make for you. Other people may be able to point out the pros and cons and the consequences. Friends and family might be able to explain some reasons why you need to consider changing. However, each individual person must make the personal choice and commitment to change.

3. Reinforcement

A third key factor, a critical element in maintaining positive change, is reinforcement. This requires ongoing support and encouragement to make that commitment last. Without ongoing reinforcement, the pitfalls will prevail. The payoffs will tend to loom. The neurotic paradox is going to be there when you're starting to feel some anxiety, tension, or discomfort. You're going to remember that relief can be almost instantaneous. Euphoric recall is going to kick in when you think back on past experiences and you'll tend to remember how good it felt, the positive points. You'll tend to forget the negative aspects.

One avenue of reinforcement is through study and self-analysis, by researching and reflecting on the nature of your predicament. Another means of reinforcement is through involvement in support groups, such as the Twelve Step programs like Alcoholics Anonymous (A.A.), where you're involved with other positive people who can support and reinforce your commitment. Counseling, therapy and personal coaching can also provide powerful reinforcement and help one to avoid the pitfalls. A combination of these types of support, encouragement, and reinforcement can be very effective. There is no easy way, no shortcuts. It takes a lot of hard work, and ongoing reinforcement is a critical element in maintaining one's commitment.

4. Develop Positive Patterns

A fourth key factor for lasting change in personal development and self-improvement is developing positive attitudes and actions. By developing and nurturing life-enhancing ways of thinking and acting we can displace the toxic patterns. By reading, studying and practicing personal development programs (such as Dr. Dan's programs *On Emotional Intelligence – Successful Personality* and *On Real-Life Intelligence – The Edge For Successful Living*) one can develop ways of being which are empowering, that free a person to function more effectively, to thrive and prosper, and to be more successful in personal and professional endeavors.

Success Over
Stress & Burnout

By "Dr. Dan" Matzke, PhD

FAQ's Addressed In This Program:

What are the main causes of stress and burnout?
How can stress be effectively managed and
burnout prevented?
Why is it so difficult to say "no" to stressful demands?
How do toxic attitudes affect stress levels?

Table of Contents

Success Over Stress & Burnout:
Introduction - Definition of Terms

This program explores powerful thoughts, ideas and practical suggestions for successfully dealing with stress and burnout. Let's begin with some working definitions of these key terms:

STRESS: 1.) Any change, positive or negative, requiring an adaptation or adjustment. 2.) A state of pressure, tension, conflict or "demand".

BURNOUT: 1.) A state of physical and mental exhaustion, which occurs as a result of too much stress, 2.) Often caused by excessively striving to attain unrealistic expectations, imposed by one's self, or by value trends in society.

SUCCESS: 1.) To succeed in one's endeavors, the attainment of desired results. 2.) To turn out well, to thrive, prosper and flourish.

Keys to Managing Stress
& Preventing Burnout

I. Be Selective - Practice Saying "Yes" to Yourself

Perhaps the most common cause of the stress & burnout phenomenon is being overcommitted and overextended. This frequently involves "trying to do too many things at once", or "having too many irons in the fire". For the compulsively driven perfectionist, it is often related to "trying to do everything equally well (perfectly)". There is a need to be selective in life, to limit the number of demands, or the amount of change, which is occurring in life.

An example may be the Sunday newspaper, which is sometimes three inches thick. If you feel obligated to read the entire paper, because you paid a dollar for it, it'll probably take you all week. Most people, however, are selective in what they read. Generally a person picks two or three sections which they are most interested in, oftentimes the comics first to set the tone for the day, and then share the rest with other family members, such as the cat or dog, who may have their favorite sections.

Most people feel OK about saying "no" to some sections of the paper, without feeling guilty. And so it is with other aspects of life. We need to periodically review our priorities, to decide what is really valuable, worthwhile, and personally meaningful to us. We need to be selective so as to limit the number of demands which we place on our self, and the number we allow others to place on us. This is the process of "pacing" one's self, so you don't burnout, and it means that you sometimes have to say "no". To say "no" to someone or something is actually saying "yes" to yourself (You're worth it, aren't you?).

This requires that we accept and respect some of our limits - physical, mental and emotional limits - as well as time, energy and financial limits. A toxic attitude which makes it especially difficult to "be selective" at times is the notion of "More is Better". This frequently leads to an escalating spiral of demands, and a sense of "time urgency", which is often the core factor in stress and burnout. (For a full discussion of this toxic attitude see Dr. Dan's program on *Success Over Stinkin' Thinkin'*.)

II. Take Action on Demands - Don't Stew, Do!!!

A key factor in effectively dealing with the real demands in life and preventing burnout is taking action on the demands. It's useless to just "stew" about them, so "do" something with them. The first step is to devise a plan of action. Having a daily, weekly and monthly schedule, or calendar of events, can be a very effective tool. This allows you to budget your time, money, appointments, social events, and leisure time. Some people also want to include time to "worry", so if that's part of your nature, why not include time for that too.

Just the process of writing things down results in a lowering of anxiety and tension levels. It reduces some of the pressure, since you no longer have to worry about forgetting something. It is very helpful for getting a clearer view of the "big picture", which allows you to see how everything can fit in, or work.

It is especially critical to plan for periods of high demand, such as tax time, end of school semesters, and major tests or evaluations. Taking action on demands, through devising a plan, budget, or schedule, helps in seeing "the light at the end of the tunnel" (not the train). This results in a realistic sense of hope that one can effectively deal with the demands, and experience success with stress.

An ounce of stress prevention is worth a pound of burnout cure. Planning, forethought, and discipline are powerful tools for successfully maintaining balance and perspective, in the face of stress and burnout.

III. Take Care of Yourself - There's Only One of You

High stress levels result in an impaired ability to focus, concentrate, and pay attention. Being more absent minded and forgetful are common symptoms of being over-stressed and burned-out. This increases the risk of having accidents and being injured, so there is a need for extra caution when involved in high risk activities such as driving, yard work, and sports. It may be wise to avoid very high risk activities when under extremely high demand/stress levels, such as rock-climbing, hang gliding, or long freeway trips.

The risk for illness also increases with high stress levels, due in part to impairment of the immune system, the body's ability to fight off germs and viruses. When the repair system is impaired, many major diseases can develop, such as cancer.

High stress and demand levels require additional rest and sleep to allow the body time to rejuvenate. Tiredness is often the first early warning sign that signals burnout is approaching. So take heed, and take care of yourself by getting adequate rest and good nutrition, using moderation with alcohol and junk food.

A second aspect of taking care of your self involves allowing time to be with your self.... for some quiet time. These quiet moments can be used to reflect on how your life is unfolding, to review priorities, and to decide what really matters to you. This is sometimes referred to as "mental health time", and some psychologists are now recommending "mental health" days off from work. While not all managers and supervisors are in agreement with this concept, it can be very preventative. By taking a day or two off work to catch up on some much needed rest, major illnesses and disorders may be avoided.

Having regular "attitude adjustments" or "emotional tune-ups", can be another way of taking care of your self. Talking with a counselor, therapist or personal life coach can be very helpful in maintaining balance and perspective.

IV.   Take Time for Play - It's a Need, Not Just a Nicety

Oftentimes during periods of high stress, play or recreation is the first thing to go out of a person's life. Play is a critical necessity and a need, not just an extra nicety. Examples of play or fun "time-outs" may include such simple things as reading for pleasure, visiting with friends, or any noncompetitive sport or activity. One word of caution - if you are under a high stress level, it is not a good time to take up a new form of play or recreation. This would be another demand or adjustment, which would increase your already high risk level for accidents and illnesses. So it wouldn't be a good idea to attempt to free your self of stress through learning skydiving, for example.

An underlying toxic attitude which makes it difficult for many people to play and relax is related to the work ethic of "I'm OK - (Only) When I'm Working". The subtle, implied message here is that "I'm Not OK - When I'm Not Working". This results in many people feeling guilty for taking "time off" or "doing nothing". Recent surveys have found that many people feel that the "fun" is going out of life. We are so busy striving, achieving, progressing, and succeeding, that we have lost our appreciation of the value of play.

Stress and burnout often is the result of work and play being "out of balance". Play is a critical element in being successful with stress and burnout. It involves the process of enjoying life, delighting in the subtle aspects of nature, art and people - to feel OK about just being (play), without having a constant need to be doing (work).

V. Develop Stress Awareness - Insight Reduces Flight

Developing an understanding of factors involved in stress and burnout can be very useful in successfully maintaining balance and perspective. One step is learning to identify what pushes your "stress buttons". For some, it is being stuck in traffic that puts them on overload. It may be certain mannerisms or characteristics in people that trigger you. (Your mother-in-law or boss may have some of these.) If you work in an office, perhaps the phone ringing pushes your stress buttons, especially towards the end of the day. Through developing an awareness of these stressors, they will have less power over you.

Learning to recognize your personal early warning signs of burnout is another aspect of developing stress awareness. Feeling tired and depressed are the most frequent symptoms many people experience when over-stressed. Being bored with a lack of enthusiasm or motivation can be a sign of job burn-out. Anger and aggression are other early warning signs which many people manifest, when they're getting a little crispy around the edges.

Another aspect of stress awareness is learning to identify your "dumping" behaviors, how you project, blame, or release your stress on others. A classic example is the person who comes home after a particularly stressful day, and proceeds to slam the door, kick the dog, and yell at their spouse. While this "dumping" may result in feeling better, it isn't an effective long term way of dealing with stress.

A toxic game that many couples often play is called "If it weren't for you...", where the spouse is blamed for the stress in one's life. This is an extremely destructive form of dumping, which can quickly end a relationship.

Stress awareness can also be developed through taking an objective view of the stressful "roles" we play. This involves putting some space between your self, and your duties and functions in the world. This ability to step back, to disengage from work, social and family roles, is very powerful, and tends to lighten the load, allowing a person to proceed more effectively. An example may be where you and a co-worker are deeply involved in a task or project, and you both pause for a moment and comment "Isn't it crazy here today, what a zoo!!" You may both laugh, and then re-engage in the task at hand. When you do so, however, there is less tension. The role has less of a grip on you, and is less consuming.

Humor and laughter is very empowering. To see something that is silly, insane, paradoxical, or ironic in work or relationships, helps to develop perspective, and reminds us not to take life too seriously (since nobody can get out of it alive).

VI. Develop Ways to Relax - Regroup to Recoup

Each person needs to develop several ways to relax that work well for them, ways that can become a regular part of their daily routine. Exercise has been shown to be one of the most effective ways of relaxing. It helps to burn up the adrenalin and muscle tension which accumulates when one is stressed. Exercise has both physical and mental calming effects, especially rhythmic exercises such as brisk walking, jogging, swimming, hiking, and dancing. Regular periods of exercise, 20 to 30 minutes in length, at least three to four times per week, is a very effective way of managing stress and preventing burnout.

Two basic methods or techniques of relaxation, which can be used almost anytime, and anyplace, focus on breathing and body muscles. While there is nothing magical or mystical about these means of relaxation, they can effectively take the edge off of anxiety and tension build-up.

The first, focused breathing, is simple the process of taking several deep.... slow.... and deliberate breaths of air (fresh if possible). This momentary break tends to calm the body and the mind, resulting in a lowering of anxiety and tension levels.

A second technique of muscle relaxation, focuses on the letting go of unneeded muscle tension, which builds up over time when under stress. By deliberately tensing up muscle groups, holding it for a few seconds, and then letting the muscles relax, a person can learn to greatly lower the draining tension build up, especially in areas such as the neck, shoulders and back, which can lead to headaches.

While the two basic relaxation methods can be useful in lowering anxiety and tension levels, it is easy to forget to use them, when one gets caught up in a busy day. It is helpful to develop some reminders, or cues, to relax in your daily schedule. For example, if you have a watch that "beeps" on the hour, you may use the beep as a reminder to take a few deep breaths, and to let go of unneeded muscle tension.

In an office, the phone ringing can be used as a cue. Usually the phone ringing results in a rushed response, it's another demand to be answered. Instead, turn it into a relaxed response, taking a nice deep breath, and letting some tension out of the muscles, before answering the phone. Lunch and coffee breaks are also good times to deliberately relax, and to step out of your hectic work role. If you can put some physical space between yourself, and your place of duty, it makes mentally disengaging much easier.

Meditation is another form of relaxation which many people find effective. Simply put, meditation is the process of calming the mind, of turning off the intellect and stopping the incessant noise and chatter. This mental "time-out" can be very refreshing and rejuvenating. A simple technique which you can use the next time your mind is moving along in the fast lane, talking a mile-a-minute while you would like it to stop, is to say to your busy intellect "I'm Listening!!" Most people find that when they actually stop and listen to their hyperactive mind, it has nothing to say, it's just silent. That silence, even momentary, is meditation, and it is very beneficial to experience it on a regular basis.

The goal of relaxing is to center oneself, or to regroup. It's very easy to get caught up in being everywhere and everywhen but, here and now. This widespread epidemic is a form of "hurry sickness" in which a person feels a constant pressure to be "somewhere else". Relaxing is the process of being in the present, and enjoying it, not feeling the need to be anywhere else. This is a key factor in successfully dealing with stress and burnout.

One word of caution regarding the use of "Better Living Through Chemistry" to relax. Alcohol and drugs can be very seductive and addictive, a habit pattern which is very hard to break. They tend to reduce and impair one's ability to effectively deal with stress, and to enjoy life. (For a full discussion of this toxic attitude see Dr. Dan's program on *Success Over Stinkin' Thinkin'*.)

VII. Develop Expectation Awareness - Evaluate and Update

All of us have models of reality or mental pictures which we carry around in our minds, of how we think things should be, ought to be, or must be. These expectations often don't match the real world, how it is. The bigger the difference between our mental models or expectations of people, places and things, and how it really is (reality), the more conflict, frustration, and stress we experience.

Oftentimes we cannot change reality. There are many "givens" of existence which we need to accept, conditions such as natural catastrophes, accidents, illnesses, social customs and laws. However, we can change, modify, and/or let go of our unrealistic expectations. By developing an awareness of our expectations, we can reduce stress and conflict through adjusting and aligning our mental pictures, updating and revising them as necessary. Burnout often results from the futile attempt to live up to impossible expectations, which are self-imposed demands.

A very powerful stress reduction technique is to consciously examine and evaluate your "expectations", when you experience conflict or stress. Ask yourself "What is the picture I have in my mind of how I expect that things should or ought to be, and how is that different from the situation at hand?" With this awareness and understanding, you can then more effectively decide what to change to reduce conflict and stress: either 1) your unrealistic expectations, or 2) something in the world.

Concluding Comments – The Terrible "Shoulds"

Many times our expectations take the form of "shoulds". For example, many people are programmed to think that they "should" be a good worker, "should" be a good spouse, "should" be a good parent, "should" be a good citizen, and/or "should" be a good lover. Also, we "should" be kind and understanding, and we "should" be tolerant and polite. We are bombarded with "should" after "should" after "should", and after awhile you can get tired of being "should" upon.

So, it's important not to "should" on yourself, and not to let other people "should" on you either.

In summary, it's been said that "I've never met a person who has given me as much trouble as myself." We are often our own worst enemy, causing much of our own stress through having unrealistic expectations and self-imposed demands on your self, leading to burnout. So, "If you want enlightenment (a sense of peace and serenity), then lighten up (stop "shoulding" on yourself). Keep your expectations in check.

Success Over Stinkin' Thinkin'

By "Dr. Dan" Matzke, PhD

FAQ's Addressed In This Program:

What is Stinkin' Thinkin'?
How does Stinkin' Thinkin' affect one's actions?
Why are these toxic attitudes so difficult to change?
What are the steps for shrinkin' stinkin' thinkin'?

Table Of Contents

Introduction:
The Nature of Stinkin' Thinkin'

Common Toxic Attitudes, Myths & Illusions:
More Is Better
It'll Be Better...Later
I'm OK - (Only) When I'm Working
Better Living Through Chemistry
I Must Be In Control
If I Fail - Then I Am A Failure
I Must Excel At Everything I Do
I Must Not Offend Anyone
Life Should Be Fair
Life Owes Me
Yes But/What If
Ideal Expectations

Keys to Shrinkin' Stinkin' Thinkin'

Success Over Stinkin' Thinkin':
Introduction - The Nature of Stinkin' Thinkin'

This program explores "Stinkin' Thinkin'" — toxic attitudes and self-defeating behaviors. Let's begin with a story that demonstrates a relatively mild example of Stinkin' Thinkin'. This is a story about a young couple who were preparing a Sunday afternoon dinner. The husband and wife were in the kitchen, and the husband was watching his wife prepare a ham. He noticed that she took the ham, and cut about an inch or so off the end of it, and then laid both pieces in a pan. He asked his wife, "Why did you cut the end of the ham off like that? What is the purpose of doing that?" The wife thought about it for a while and really couldn't come up with any logical reasons why she cut the end of the ham off. All she could think of was that her Mother always used to do that and she learned it from her.

Well, some time later the couple was together with the Mother-in-law and the Mother-in-law was fixing ham for dinner. The husband was watching her and, sure enough, she took the ham, cut about an inch or so off the end, put the ham and the little extra piece in a pan, and put it in the oven. He asked her, "You know, your daughter cuts the end of the ham off like that, puts it on the side in a pan. I notice that you do that, too. Your daughter really couldn't think of any reasons why she cut the end off like that, other than you had taught her to do it. I notice that you do it. Why? What's the purpose of that?" The Mother-in-law thought about it for a while, and she couldn't think of any reasons why she cut the end of the ham off either, other than her Mother used to do it and she learned it from her.

Well it happened that the Grandmother was still alive and the family all got together for a holiday one time. The husband was watching and the Grandmother was preparing a ham also. She just took the whole ham, stuck it in a pan, and put it in the oven. Well, this really perplexed the husband. He asked the Grandmother, "Your daughter and your granddaughter both cut the end of their ham off, about an inch or so, lay that on the side in the pan, and then put it in the oven. I have asked both of them why they do that, and they can't think of any logical reason or purpose for cutting the end of the ham off. They both said they learned it from you. In watching you, I noticed that you don't do that. You just put the whole ham in the pan and stick it in the oven." The Grandmother thought about it for a few moments, and kind of smiled and said, "I used to cut the end of the ham off. That was because I had a small pan and the ham wouldn't all fit in it. Now I have a larger pan, and I don't need to cut the end of the ham off any more."

This is a somewhat humorous example of how ways of thinking and responding to situations are oftentimes passed down from generation to generation. Along this progression, sometimes, they are no longer needed. Some times they are no longer appropriate, or sometimes they become somewhat self-defeating or useless. In this particular example, there weren't any major problems that were caused by continuing to cut the end of the ham off —

perhaps only that the piece got a little bit dried out or crispy in the cooking.

However, in other areas of life, there are toxic attitudes, myths and illusions in life that sometimes get passed down from generation to generation which leads to more serious self-defeating and sabotaging behaviors. This program takes a look at common forms of Stinkin' Thinkin' that are perpetuated and reinforced in our society by the media, by peers, and by value trends. It explores toxic attitudes, myths, and illusions which lead to self-defeating behaviors, and it reviews the keys to shrinkin' stinkin' thinkin'.

Common Forms of *Stinkin' Thinkin'* –
Toxic Attitudes, Myths & Illusions

1.   "More Is Better"

One of the most common forms of Stinkin' Thinkin', a very toxic attitude that is quite prevalent in our society and culture, is the notion that "more is better." Regardless of how much I have, no matter where I am at, if I had more, I would be happier. If I had more, I would be more satisfied. More is better. If I could do it faster, quicker, higher, longer, larger, if I could be richer, it would be better. More is better.

This attitude expresses itself in many different areas of life. One common area in which this attitude is expressed is in regard to food. If I have one little chocolate chip cookie for dessert, somehow two would be better. More is better. If I have two chocolate chip cookies, perhaps two dozen would be even better. More is better. If I have one beer on a hot Sunday afternoon, then perhaps two beers would be better. If I have a six-pack of beer for a holiday weekend, somehow perhaps a twelve-pack of beer would be even better. More is better.

The same thinking applies in the realm of money. If you are working and managing on $10 an hour, there's the notion in the back of one's mind that "more is better." If I could manage to earn $15 an hour, then perhaps I could be even more happy, more satisfied. So you strive and achieve, and get promotion, and you start earning $15 an hour. That idea is still there -- that Stinkin' Thinkin' is still operating. More is better. If I could earn let's say $20 an hour, that would be better still. So you strive, and achieve, and get another promotion, and you start earning $20 an hour. The Stinkin' Thinkin' is still there. More is better. The idea becomes if I could just earn $25 an hour, then I'd be really happy. Striving for more and more to be happy, always striving, but never arriving.

The problem with this "more is better" attitude is that one can continue to strive, and to reach endlessly, and can go through a whole lifetime never really reaching a place where you feel good about where you're at, or feel good about what you have. It's important, at times, to step out of this progression and take a break from this "more is better" attitude - to take some time out to enjoy the fruits of one's labor, to appreciate what one has and where one is. To, at various points in life, spend some time on a plateau. To feel good about, to feel content with, to feel peace with, where you're at, what you have, and the progress you have made.

2.   "It'll Be Better...Later"

A second form of Stinkin' Thinkin' that's very common in our society is the myth or notion that "it'll be better...later". At some point in the future I'll be happier, I'll be satisfied, I'll be more content. Right now isn't going too well or it's just so-so. This is expressed in many different areas. If you're feeling alone and isolated, there may be the notion that it will be better later, once I find the perfect person out there, once I find my match, once I find my mate. There are some romantic notions and myths that when you find this perfect person and get married, it will be better. It will be better later, once I get married. If you are married and you're in a relationship that isn't working very well, you may believe that it'll be better later, once you get your divorce. It'll be better once you get rid of this person and have your freedom again.

The same notion is often expressed when a person is looking at different places and different things. If only I had this, if only I were to live there, when I have this, when I get to move there, then I'll be happier, then I'll be satisfied.

The problem with this belief is that the primary focus is some time off in the future, some place off in the distance. It is living in a fantasy world. The person is being "everywhere" and "everywhen" except here and now. When a person's focus and emphasis is on the future, it tends to rob a person of the ability to appreciate the present, to appreciate what is, to appreciate the here and now. It is very easy for a person to go through his whole lifetime with this notion, "It will be better later, it will be better some time in the future."

This often happens with people in their work and their careers. They're involved in a job that they don't really enjoy, don't feel good about. But in the back of their mind is the notion, "It'll be better later, once I retire." Now I'm going to work, now I'm going to struggle, I'm going to save my money, I'm going to invest, because once I reach retirement (if I reach retirement), then I'll be happy, then I'll be satisfied. It often happens that a person works, strives, saves, invests, and when they do reach retirement, they find that they are not happy. It is not better. And there is disappointment. Many people often die before they reach that time, somewhere down the road, that illusionary "later."

It'll be better...later, is a form of Stinkin' Thinkin' that has some negative side effects, which robs a person of the ability to enjoy the present, to appreciate what is, here and now.

3.   "I'm OK - (Only) When I'm Working"

A third toxic attitude that is very prevalent in our society and culture is the myth of "I'm OK - (Only) When I'm Working". When I'm striving, when I'm achieving, when I'm succeeding, when I'm progressing, then I'm OK, I'm of value, and I'm of worth. Our American society and culture was built on this work ethic, that we as a person are of value and are of worth when we're working.

This "I'm OK when I'm working" is valid. It has an appropriate time and place. The difficulty occurs because it is very seductive and addictive. It's true that I'm OK when I'm working. There is also a sense that the more work I do, the more OK I am ("more is better"). It is very easy to get hooked on this as a sole source of satisfaction and self-validation.

I'm OK (only) when I'm working, and the more work I do the more OK I am often leads into becoming a workaholic, where a person's primary or sole source of satisfaction is through the area of work. A person may lose his appreciation, his value of, relationships and play. The "I'm OK (Only) When I'm Working" myth often leads to a sense of "time urgency". I just don't have enough time to get all the work done that I think I should, or ought to get done. There is also a subtle implied message here that "I'm not OK when I'm not working." This results in a person having difficulty in playing and relaxing. There is a sense of guilt that I should be working. I'm OK when I'm working, and if I'm not working, there is something wrong with me. If I'm not producing, if I'm not contributing, if I'm not striving and achieving, then I'm not of value, I'm not of worth.

It's important that we take time to step out of our work roles and allow ourselves to enjoy some other areas of life. These include our relationships and play. It is critical not to feel a constant need to be "doing" something all the time, and to be able to enjoy just the process of "being", without feeling guilty.

4.   "Better Living Through Chemistry"

A fourth form of Stinkin' Thinkin' with very powerful negative consequences and self-defeating behaviors is the notion that better living can be accomplished through chemistry. If you have any aches and pains, if you're feeling tension or stress or conflict, then there is some chemical way of dealing with that. "Better living through chemistry." Our society is a pain-denying society. We tend to find all sorts of ways of managing or reducing pain, stress, conflict, ways of dealing with these symptoms so that we're pain-free, comfortable and happy. This is available through a wide variety of chemical means including alcohol, drugs, and prescription medications. Many commercials on TV talk about pain management, about better living through chemistry. If you're feeling muscle aches and pains, if you're feeling tension headaches, there's bound to be some type of aspirin or pain relief medication you can take to feel better fast, to get instant relief.

"Better living through chemistry" is also promised with alcohol. If you've been working and really having a rough day, a lot of pressure, then why not stop off for happy hour? Why not stop off and have a little attitude adjustment period, get some relief, get some satisfaction, get some pleasure, and feel good? It's Miller Time. This Bud's for You. Have yourself a Henry's.

Street drugs also appeal to the idea of better living through chemistry. Cocaine, for example, has a glamour image of being in the fast lane, having a lot of energy, power, sex and money. "Better living through chemistry" can be very attractive. Amphetamines and speed also appeal to this notion. If you need a little extra lift, if you're working overtime, if you need a little something to get you through a difficult period of time, try a line or two of speed, put a little crank in your coffee. It will give you that extra energy, that extra lift that you need to make it through the long day or night shift.

The medical profession, through prescription drugs, also buys into "better living through chemistry." If you're having any kind of ache or pain, any kind of stress or tension, there is some chemical way of managing those, some chemical way of dealing with that conflict. Looking at various prescription drugs, there is Librium to liberate you, Valium to validate you, and Elavil to elevate you -- chemical ways of helping you to feel better.

The problem with better living through chemistry is that it tends to focus on symptoms. It takes a shortcut to feeling good, to relieving pain. It tends to ignore the real causes and problems.

Better living through chemistry is a toxic attitude that can lead to some very self-defeating behaviors, with chemical dependency and addiction being some of the side effects and consequences that are very difficult to change.

5.   "I Must Be In Control"

A fifth common form of Stinkin' Thinkin' in our society and culture is the myth that "I must be in control" — I must be in control of everything all of the time. This leads to some desperate attempts to plan, organize, and schedule everything, to maintain this sense of being in control. To set up some deadlines, criteria, standards of performance that lead to the illusion, at least, of being in control.

This belief is also expressed in the desire or need to feel that one has all of the answers all of the time. I must be in control. I must have all of the answers. If you're a parent, a boss, a supervisor, or a teacher and you have the notion that "I must be in control", you'll have a great deal of difficulty at times in saying, "I don't know", or "I'm not sure." This myth "I must be in control" may also be expressed in the area of controlling one's feelings and emotions. Don't let them show, keep them inside. Men traditionally have been programmed with the notion that they really shouldn't show affection, they shouldn't be soft or caring. It's OK to show anger. It's OK to show aggression. But any type of gentleness or caring should be controlled. Certainly a man should not cry. Women, on the other hand, have traditionally been programmed that it's OK for them to show caring and affection, it's OK for them to cry, but it's really inappropriate for them to get upset, to get mad. They should be able to control those feelings.

The "I must be in control" of everything all of the time belief also may be expressed as an attempt to control oneself physically, trying to control one's sicknesses or illnesses. If you've bought into this notion and you get a cold or the flu or diarrhea, you may feel that I should be able to control this. It really isn't that bad. I really need to go into work. One day you may have diarrhea and feel that "I should be in control" and "I'm OK - (Only) When I'm Working", so you pucker up and go to the job. With the myth that I must be in control of everything all of the time, a person runs into a great deal of conflict, and a great deal of frustration, when they encounter some of the gray areas of life. Some of those areas in life where there's a lot of ambiguity. If you hang on to this notion that I must be in control, when you encounter some of the disorder, the doubt, and uncertainty in life, you'll experience a great deal of anxiety, a great deal of uneasiness. When you encounter situations in which there are no guarantees, when you can't be sure of yourself, when you must take some risk, if you're indoctrinated or programmed with this notion that I must be in control, you are going to experience a lot of frustration.

The notion that "I must be in control" tends to lead to an elevated level of stress. A person often sets up some unrealistic demands and expectations on themselves, setting up some impossible schedules, standards, and deadlines that tend to aggravate stress that can lead to the burn-out syndrome. "I must be in control" is a toxic attitude that results in frustration and self-defeating behaviors.

6.   "If I Fail, Then I Am A Failure"

A sixth example of Stinkin' Thinkin' is the attitude of "If I fail, then I am a failure" — if I fail at something that I try, then I am a failure as a person. If we attempt two or three different things in life and they don't happen to work out, we're not successful at them, it's very easy to get into that rut of thinking that "Gee, I have failed, therefore I as a person have failed, then I'm not very good, I'm not competent, I'm not very successful." If you view failures from that perspective, from the attitude that "If I fail then I am a failure", this tends to reduce a person's self-confidence and self-esteem. When you're faced with future tasks and future challenges, you're likely to feel less able to take on those challenges, less able to function effectively.

In reality, there's a general 60/40 rule that exists. Most people are usually successful, are usually able to accomplish things on the first try only about 60% of the time. About 40% of the time they're unsuccessful, they're a failure, it doesn't work. If you look at a lot of the top-rated teams in different sports, actually they win only about 60 of their games, they lose about 40.   In some areas, this example is taken to a further extreme. If you look at baseball, if someone is batting an average of 300, he's doing quite well. That means that 70 of the time that a person goes to the plate, he's a failure, he doesn't get a hit. So the 60/40 ratio is a good rule of thumb to keep in mind, indicating that in life much of the time we're not successful, much of the time we fail, about 40%.

The "If I fail, then I'm a failure" attitude is very toxic, resulting in reduced self-esteem, reduced self-confidence, and feelings of hopelessness for the future. It's important to look at unsuccessful experiences as an opportunity to grow. What is it that I can learn from this non-success? What lesson can I glean from this experience so that I can be better prepared in the future for similar tasks and challenges that I will encounter? Questions like these tend to clear one's thinkin', and to increase personal effectiveness.

7.   "I Must Excel At Everything I Do"

A seventh example of Stinkin' Thinkin' is the attitude of I must excel at everything I do. I must be outstanding, I must be the best. This includes the perfectionistic attitude that many people have - that if I'm going to do anything, it's going to be perfect, it's going to be the best. There's an all-or-nothing approach that develops — either I'm going to do it, I'm going to do it all the way, I'm going to do it perfect, or I'm not going to do it at all, I'm not going to even give it a try.

With the idea that I must excel at everything I do, comes the external reference that I have to live up to other people's expectations, I have to live up to other people's standards, I need their approval, I need others' acceptance. There's a lack of trust or valuing of one's own processing, of one's own enjoyment of the activity. The person is missing the process of doing something and is more concerned about other people's evaluations, approval and opinions.

"I must excel at everything I do, I must be outstanding, I must be the best," is saying that if I can't do it perfectly, then I'm just going to forget about it, that I don't want to do it at all. The humorous saying of "It's OK to be So - So", points to the fact that we don't always have to excel, we don't have to be perfect at everything we do. Most people have one or two areas in their life that they perform very well. It's important to allow ourselves to do some things to our own satisfaction, to our own delight, to do it just for the enjoyment of doing it, without having to feel the need to do it perfectly or to excel at it.

8.   "I Must Not Offend Anyone"

An eighth common example of Stinkin' Thinkin' is the attitude of "I must not offend anyone." This involves slipping into the rut of being non-assertive and passive. "I must not offend anyone" would include notions such as "Don't rock the boat," "Don't make any waves", "Don't hurt anyone's feelings." The idea is that everything must go smoothly, that we shouldn't have any conflicts or clashes, we don't want to ruffle anyone's feathers. In reality, it's difficult to go through life without offending a few people, without confronting people with the fact that perhaps they're violating some of our rights, they're infringing upon us, taking advantage or using us. Anyone who has tried to raise children knows that it's relatively impossible to do that without offending them at times, without confronting them, without setting some limits.

The "I must not offend anyone" attitude results in a person being self-sacrificing, by being passive, allowing themselves to be used, taken advantage of, or to be manipulated. That takes a toll, and has a price. Now this doesn't mean that we have to go around offending people just for the sport or the fun of it. It does mean, though, at certain times it's appropriate and needed to offend people, to take a stand, to confront them.

9.   "Life Should Be Fair"

A ninth example of Stinkin' Thinkin' is the myth that "Life should be fair."   This is an attitude that is often expressed during adolescence – "that's not fair" - it's not fair that I have to be in by 10:00 at night. My friends don't have to be in until 1:00 in the morning. Or it's not fair that I have to do my homework in the evening - none of the other kids do theirs.

There are many laws, rules, regulations, and policies and procedures in our society and culture that aren't always fair, that don't always balance out. If a person clings to this notion that life should be fair, they're likely to encounter a great deal of frustration and disappointment.

Another area of life that is not always fair is when we're confronted with having illnesses, or being involved in accidents. The question often arises, "Why me?" It's not fair that this should happen to me.   Again, if you cling to the notion that "life should be fair", that everybody should be treated equally, you're likely to be disappointed.

Recognizing and accepting that we do not live in a "just world" is a key step in breaking through the illusion that "Life should be fair".

10.   "Life Owes Me"

A tenth example of Stinkin' Thinkin' is the notion that "Life Owes Me." This is expressed in many different areas. One example might be how children often look at their parents and say, "You owe me some things." You owe me an allowance, you owe me certain privileges, I deserve it, I don't have to work for it, I don't have to earn it, my parents owe me, or life owes me.

Oftentimes students will look at a school in this way — the school owes me an education. I deserve it - I don't have to work for it, I don't have to put effort into learning how to read and write - the school owes me a diploma.

Governments struggle with the idea of whether or not it owes its people a certain standard of living. Does it owe its people certain rights and privileges, or do the people need to work for them, do they need to earn them, do they need to invest some time and energy to get what they want?

This notion that "life owes me" results in a great deal of conflict and frustration when a person gets out into the world and discovers that we generally get what we earn. We really have to work for most things in life.

11.   "Yes But/What If"

Another form of Stinkin' Thinkin' can be referred to as the "Yes But/What If" syndrome. The "yes but-er" person is the individual who will acknowledge that there are some positive, enjoyable aspects in life, but tends to negate those and focus on the negative -- what is not, or what can't be. The "yes but-er" will discount any kind of suggestions, guidance or advice that you might be able to offer, and just dwell on the misery.

The "what if-er" is the person who has all sorts of catastrophic expectations, that tends to focus on doom and gloom, with an emphasis on the negative. What if there's an earthquake? What if I'm in an accident? What if I get some type of illness? What if I forget? What if I fail? The "what if-er" endlessly comes up with failure, or catastrophic occurrences which may happen, but which are often unlikely.

The "Yes But/What If" syndrome tends to focus on negative aspects of life at the exclusion of the positive qualities of reality. A common example would be if you were to get into your car and start it up and notice that the gas gauge, as it stabilized, was pointed right in the middle. The question is whether that gas tank is half-full or half-empty. Your attitude toward this gas tank, how you perceive it, will affect your reactions, your emotional response to this real situation. If your focus, your attitude, is that the gas tank is half-empty, (Yes - I have half a tank - But, it's half empty — what if I run out?), it is likely that you're going to have a lot of negative reactions. If your focus is on that it's half-empty, you might start thinking of all the things you can't do because the tank is half-empty. Perhaps you can't take a trip down to the beach, perhaps you can't go bumming around and visiting some friends, perhaps you won't be able to go spend some money on a new outfit because you have to put some money in the gas tank. You might get so frustrated and so discouraged because you're focusing on the fact that the gas tank is half-empty that you might just turn the car off, go back in the house, and take up "better living through chemistry."

If, on the other hand, you focus on the fact that the gas tank is half-full, it is much more likely that you're going to have some positive reactions. You might start thinking of all the things you can do with a half-tank of gas - all the opportunities, all the potential things that can occur, with a half-tank of gas. Perhaps you could go out job hunting, find some work, earn some money, and fill the gas tank up.

By choosing which side of the needle we're going to focus on, we are able to select what type of reactions we're going to have, to select our emotional response. We as human beings are able to focus and direct our attention on what we're going to emphasize, what's going to be of most value and importance to us. This form of Stinkin' Thinkin', this "yes but/what if" approach, has a great deal of influence on our emotional state, our responses, our reactions. If we choose to focus on the more positive aspects of life, the side effects are that we're going to have a much more satisfying, pleasant, and hopeful outlook overall.

12.   "Ideal Expectations"

A twelfth example of Stinkin' Thinkin' can be referred to as having "Ideal Expectations" from life. One example of this might be the American Dream, which is perpetuated in television, magazines and movies. The American Dream describes what a family is like - a happy couple living together with two or three healthy children, having their own home, able to take trips and to have vacations. As children grow they are programmed with this information. Television, movies, and magazines develop these ideal expectations. In reality, the majority of families and homes do not work this way. There are a lot of families that don't have happy couples. All children aren't healthy. Many families cannot afford their own home. Most couples are working and are busy striving and saving. Trips and vacations are few and far between. The family picture is often very different from the ideal model portrayed.

Another area of ideal expectations that's perpetuated through the media is the notion of romantic love. All sorts of illusions and fantasies of what it's going to be like when I meet the perfect person, when I meet my mate. Bells will go off, chimes will ring, and the earth will shake when I meet the ideal person, when I fall in love. And then when a person meets somebody and I gets married they discover that it isn't anywhere near like it was in the movies, romance novels or TV. A big difference often exists between ideal expectations and reality.

Ideal expectations include unrealistic expectations, standards, and demands - models that we develop in our head of how it should be, or ought to be. What happens is that when we encounter reality, we find that it's often quite different from some of our ideal expectations, that the real world is several notches away from the ideal models that we carry in our mind.

The bigger the gap is between our ideal expectations and reality, the more disappointment and frustration. Having "ideal expectations", unrealistic mental models, standards, and demands, is a form of Stinkin' Thinkin' that results in a great deal of stress and conflict. The key to overcoming this illusion is developing an awareness of our "ideal expectations", the pictures in our head of how we were programmed to think things should be, ought to be, or must be. With this awareness and understanding, we can revise, update, and/or let go of, our unrealistic mental models, and come to a greater acceptance of what is and what can be.

Shrinkin' Stinkin' Thinkin' – Takin' C.A.R.E.

A response pattern of attitudes and behaviors can be outlined which helps to clarify how our "Stinkin' Thinkin'" affects our actions.

1. Conditions & Circumstances

Imagine a scene where a person is walking down a street and notices a dog approaching.

2. Attitudes & Assumptions

Each individual carries with them a set of attitudes and assumptions about dogs, which they learned and developed over the years. Some of these may include "Dogs are friends," or "Dogs bite."

3. Reactions & Responses

How a person reacts or responds to a given set of Conditions & Circumstances is based on the Attitudes & Assumptions he has learned and developed. If a person grew up in a family with dogs as pets, they may have developed an attitude of "Dogs are friends", and their emotional reactions to seeing a dog approaching may be warmth and affection. Their response may be to pause for a few minutes and pet the dog.

On the other hand, if a person was frightened by a dog as a child, and/or bitten, they probably developed the attitude that dogs are to be avoided and the assumption that all dogs bite. The emotional reaction of this person is likely to be fear, and the response may be to look for a way to get away from the dog.

These Reactions & Responses are automatic and habitual, with little or no conscious thought involved. When we learn and develop Attitudes & Assumptions which are toxic, ineffective, or inappropriate, the results are Reactions & Responses which may be self-defeating, sabotaging and frustrating.

4. Examine & Evaluate

The key to changing Stinkin' Thinkin', attitudes which don't work or which are toxic, is to Examine & Evaluate them. Through developing awareness and understanding of our Attitudes & Assumptions, we are able to reprogram ourselves with more effective and satisfying thoughts, ideas, and perspectives.

Conditions & Circumstances
Attitudes & Assumptions
Reactions & Responses
Examine & Evaluate

To take "CARE" of oneself involves taking charge of one's thinking - to look at it objectively, with detachment, to ferret out the stinkin' thinkin', which impairs and inhibits personal growth and development, and is a detriment to our effectiveness and well-being.

Maintaining Perspective on Stinkin' Thinkin'

It's important to maintain a sense of perspective regarding these different examples of Stinkin' Thinkin'. There is a grain of truth in many of them. There are places where they apply, times when they're appropriate, where these ideas, values and beliefs function effectively.

For example, the idea of "Better Living Through Chemistry" has indeed helped the human condition through such chemical breakthroughs as the vaccine for polio and antibiotics such as penicillin. The "I'm OK - When I'm Working" value is very valid, and most people derive a great deal of personal satisfaction from their work and careers, which also contribute to the welfare of society. The belief of "More Is Better" is also appropriate as it applies to more caring, more respect and more patience.

It's important then that we have a degree of awareness and appreciation of how these ideas can apply, and when they can work. It's also important that we understand how attitudes, myths, and illusions can become very toxic and self-defeating when they're misapplied, when we habitually respond and rigidly use these in life situations where they don't work. Stinkin' Thinkin' is often the result of using valid ideas as universal imperatives; absolute shoulds, oughts, or musts. A person is better able to guide and direct their life in more effective and satisfying ways, through maintaining balance and perspective.

On Emotional Intelligence
Successful Personality

By "Dr. Dan" Matzke, PhD

FAQ's Addressed In This Program:

What is emotional intelligence?
What are the key elements of a successful personality?
How do these characteristics result
in a person being more effective?
Why are negative personality patterns
so difficult to change?
What are the steps for developing more successful
attitudes & actions?

Table of Contents

Preface/Introduction: On Emotional Intelligence - Successful Personality

What is "emotional intelligence"? Emotional intelligence refers to an awareness of and ability to manage emotions and create motivation. It is a set of personal and interpersonal skills (including the ability to apply knowledge & understanding) related to one's personality and behavior patterns, which results in a person being able to function more effectively in life.

This program explores twelve key elements of "Successful Personality" which promote personal effectiveness and well-being. The word "personality" refers to an individual's total make-up, including psychological and emotional characteristics, and behavior. The phrase "successful personality" refers to an individual who is highly functioning, who is well-adjusted, a person who is effective at living – thriving & prosperous. They would tend to have a high level of self-esteem and self-confidence, a sense of purpose and direction in life, and would feel that they are being productive, useful, and contributing to the world around them. Characteristics of successful personality tend to minimize stinkin' thinkin' and to maximize effective thinking. These traits of successful personality can be developed through study and practice, thereby increasing an individual's personal and professional success in life. Let's begin by stating that no one individual has all of theses characteristics all of the time, but we can all work toward developing them more in our lives. The key elements aren't presented in any particular order or priority - rather they tend to overlap and interact with each other, much like the strands of a rope.

Twelve Power Points For A Successful Personality

1.   Openness

One aspect of successful personality necessary for effective functioning is a sense of openness, a willingness to see how it is. This sense of openness involves having accurate perceptions of reality, a clear view, and an openness to one's inner experiences as well as the outer world. This requires openness to feedback from our interactions with the world, which is essential for learning from our experiences. Openness includes a willingness to express oneself, to clearly put out what one thinks, what one feels, one's point of view, hopes, dreams, needs and desires. It also includes an openness to listen to, and hear, other points of view, opinions, other people's needs, wants, and desires. Openness includes an accurate self-concept, to see your self clearly, to be able to see what one's own skills, talents and abilities are, as well as one's faults and weaknesses.

This sense of openness requires a minimal use of psychological defense mechanisms. These are screens and filters which we tend to use to keep out different aspects of reality which are unpleasant to look at. One of the most basic forms of a psychological defense mechanism is that of denial, a refusal to look at unpleasant facts or conditions. An example would be a child that is discovered in the kitchen with cookie crumbs on his lips, and when a parent asks the child "Have you been eating cookies?", the child would deny that he has been anywhere near the cookie jar, refusing to look at and acknowledge the evidence.

Adults oftentimes use denial with chemical dependency, refusing to look at the negative side effects or consequences of drug and alcohol use. Smoking is another area where denial is used on a massive scale, and we as a society and culture for various economic reasons, deny the negative consequences, refusing to acknowledge the lethal reality.

A second example of a common psychological defense mechanism is that of projection. In this process, a person projects his thoughts and feelings into other people, places or things, as a way of not owning or avoiding them. Through projection, a person will point the finger, or blame others, as opposed to being open to the fact that they are responsible or accountable for the situation at hand.

So a key element of successful personality is a sense of openness, involving a clear view of oneself and others, receptivity to feedback from our interactions with the world, and a minimal use of psychological defense mechanisms.

2.   Acceptance

A second aspect of successful personality is a sense of acceptance - acceptance of self, others, society, and nature. This includes acceptance of one's inner thoughts, feelings, needs, and desires, including one's sexuality - an acceptance of these as being a normal part of being a human. This sense of acceptance involves a basic life attitude of "I'm OK, and You're OK" - I'm of value and worth, and you're of value and worth, a feeling of mutual respect.

This would include an acceptance of limits; physical limits, psychological limits, social and legal limits. With this acceptance comes a sense of surrender, acknowledging that there are some edges or boundaries to what we're able to do. For example, one legal limit is that of speed limits. It may be that these imposed limits of our legal system are not always fair, just, or rational. They do exist, however. There's a need for acceptance of the limits. If we insist on defying or ignoring the limits, we're likely to experience some negative consequences such as fines or loss of driver's licensee. Another example of a limit in our society is that of taxes. It's easy to complain and moan about the fact that we have to pay taxes on our income, but it is part of our reality, and if we can come to accept and go with it, life can progress along a lot easier.

As a person matures and ages, there are also physical limits that come into being, we're just not able to function and perform as effectively as we did at a younger age. This sense of acceptance also includes a tolerance of personal faults, defects and weaknesses. Many people are able to tolerate faults and defects in other people, but have difficulty in accepting them in one's own self.

So an important aspect of successful personality is a sense of acceptance; acceptance of oneself, of others, of nature, and of limits.

3.   Spontaneity

A third facet of successful personality is a sense of spontaneity. This refers to a sense of aliveness, a zest for living, an enthusiasm for life. Spontaneity involves allowing our child within to have some fun, to play and enjoy life. Spontaneity includes a flexible approach to life, allowing ourselves to be spontaneous, as opposed to being over-controlled, where we rigidly try to keep everything in order, in planned sequence, in its' place.

Spontaneity also involves expressing our creativity and using our creative energies. Oftentimes creativity is just associated with the arts and music. Our creative energy can be expressed in just about everything we do. To use our imagination and creativity is an important aspect of maintaining a successful personality. A housewife, for example, might use her creative energies in working in the kitchen, in planning different menus, in how she prepares and serves the food. A person working in the yard also has opportunity to use his creativity and imagination in how he mows the lawn, how he trims the shrubbery, and how he arranges the flowers in the garden. All are subtle ways in which we are able to use and express our creativity, to be spontaneous.

Many other opportunities exist in work and play, to use one's imagination and spontaneity, to maintain this sense of aliveness and zest for living, an important element in successful personality.

4.   Autonomy

A fourth key element of successful personality is a sense of autonomy.   This refers to a freedom from being dependent, a freedom from being self-sacrificing, passive and nonassertive, of being more inner-directed.   This involves a willingness and ability to make choices, to take responsibility, and to take risks.   An autonomous person recognizes and accepts that everything that we attempt and try in life is not always going to be successful.   We're likely to fail at many things.   The autonomous person is willing to make choices, to commit oneself to them, to take responsibility, and to take risks.   An autonomous person also has a high degree of self-confidence and an inner trust in their own judgment, skills and abilities.

Oftentimes the word autonomy conjures up ideas of a person being totally independent and just doing their own thing.   This is not the case in successful personality.   An autonomous person is able to be interdependent, to be part of a team.   The autonomous person can choose to be part of a team, recognizing that as a group, often more can be accomplished than just as individuals.   The autonomous person will choose to join a team, not out of a desperate need for association, but through the realization that with teamwork, many positive things can be accomplished. An autonomous person may choose to join a team that's raising funds for a charity, for example, as opposed to choosing a team that is dealing drugs on the streets.

Being inner-directed, a willingness to take responsibility, to make choices, to take risks, an inner trust in one's own judgment, skills, and abilities - a sense of autonomy - an important element of successful personality.

5.   Trusting Relationships

A fifth key element in successful personality is the willingness and ability to have trusting relationships, a willingness to trust, to be vulnerable, and to risk honesty. This refers to the ability to have warm and caring bonds with significant other people in one's life. This would include the ability to have good communication, to connect with, and relate to, other human beings in personal and professional relationships. This does not imply that an individual with a successful personality would go around spilling his guts out to everybody he would meet, but rather that he would be able to connect with several other people, and have intimate interactions with them.

Having close, warm, and caring relationships is an important element of successful personality, which facilitates effectiveness and well-being.

6. Fellowship With Humanity

A sixth element of successful personality is a sense of fellowship with humanity. This refers to a deep identification with others and the human condition in general. This fellowship with humanity is in contrast to the "us and them" syndrome.

Any time there is an "us and them" syndrome, there are artificial walls and barriers that become established, that lead to separation and alienation between people. Having a sense of fellowship with humanity is realizing, that in reality there are no "us and them" - there's only "we"-- we the people of the planet Earth. With fellowship comes a sense of empathy, an ability and willingness to relate to other people, to be able to get into another person's shoes for awhile, to relate to how they're feeling, and what challenges they may be facing.

Relating to other individuals as human beings, with similar hopes, dreams, joys and concerns, is an important factor in successful personality.

7. Sense Of Humor

A seventh key element of successful personality is a sense of humor, the ability to laugh at oneself, and with others in a non-hostile way. A sense of humor includes the ability to appreciate some of the paradoxes and ironies of being human, of being able to poke fun at some of our human short-comings - the rather silly and foolish things that we do at times.

With a sense of humor, when we laugh, we tend to gain an objective view of life that gives us a different perspective on things. It increases our awareness and objectivity. With humor comes the ability to step out of some of our roles, our work roles and our social roles, and to see them from a new viewpoint. An example would be if you're in the middle of an argument, perhaps with your spouse, and you're really tearing at each other's throats, and something is said that strikes you both as being humorous, and for a moment or two, you both laugh and chuckle about it. When you step out of your role, your attack and counter-attack mode, oftentimes you can see the conflict from a new perspective.

When that occurs, you have a choice. From this more detached viewpoint, you can decide whether it's worthwhile continuing the foolish battle, or to stop the warring, and seek a peaceful resolution. The objectivity and perspective that one gets with a sense of humor, when laughter occurs, is very powerful. A sense of humor is a key element in successful personality.

8.   Living Here & Now

An eighth characteristic and quality of successful personality is living in the here and now, a primary focus on the present, as opposed to the past or future. Living in the here and now involves enjoying the process of an activity, enjoying the trip, valuing the experience itself, not just end products or results. Our society has become very goal   oriented,   with   an   emphasis   on   striving,

---

accomplishing, and achieving future goals in life, so much so that we've lost the ability to enjoy the process of reaching goals, of working toward end results and products, enjoying the trip. Many people report that the fun has gone out of life - that we're so busy striving, achieving and accomplishing things, that we've lost the joy of just being.

One important element of living in the present is appreciating the value of play, just experiencing life, without always having to be doing something, without always having to have a purpose, an end product, or a goal. An example of this is a family that is getting together and planning on going to the beach for a day. They rush around and get the family all gathered up and jump in the car and speed down to the beach. When they get there they find that the beach is overcast and the weather's not very pleasant for a day at the beach. So they jump back in the car and rush back home. There's a sense of the day being wasted because the beach, the end goal, wasn't satisfactory. If, on the other hand, the family had enjoyed the trip, had enjoyed the process of getting to the beach, even though the end goal didn't work out, they could have still had an enjoyable and delightful day. They may have enjoyed their time together on the drive to the beach and returning home, sharing some time together talking and listening to one another. Perhaps they just listened to the radio and enjoyed the sights on the way, taking in the nature and scenery.

An important element of successful personality is maintaining a primary focus in the here and now, participating in life, enjoying the process. Research has identified a healthy time ratio of 1:8. For each hour that an effective person spends reflecting on the past or planning for the future, they spend roughly eight hours engaged in the present, experiencing life, as opposed to thinking about it, or planning for it.

9.   Sense Of Awe & Wonder

A ninth facet of successful personality is a sense of awe and wonder. This refers to the ability to maintain one's appreciation of life's basic beauties, the subtle aspects of life that are in nature, art, and people - to be able to renew one's sense of awe and wonder. Children are a good example of this keen sense. A child may be walking along and notice a little bug on the sidewalk and get down on his hands and knees and just look at the bug, and be simply amazed at it. He might reach out to pet the bug and discover that the bug bites, and spend all sorts of time there totally intrigued by the unique aspects of the insect. We as adults might walk briskly down the sidewalk and perhaps step on the bug, with no appreciation at all for the subtle aspects of beauty within this creature.

To be able to renew one's appreciation of some of life's basic joys is another aspect. To be able to look at a sunset and appreciate it, even though you may have seen a thousand sunsets before. To be able to look at this sunset and appreciate the subtle aspects, to delight in it and enjoy it is important. Or, to be able to sit down with a person and talk with them, and listen to them, and to enjoy the conversation, even though you may have known them for twenty years. To be able to renew one's appreciation of life, and maintain a sense of awe and wonder, is an important element of successful personality.

10. Tolerance For Ambiguity

A tenth key element of successful personality is a tolerance for ambiguity. This refers to the gray areas of life. The gray area for many people is basically that time between when they're born and when they die, when they're not real sure of what's going on all of the time. A tolerance for ambiguity includes a willingness to accept disorder, indefiniteness, doubt and uncertainty as being a normal part of life - that these conditions are givens which cannot be totally overcome.

A tolerance for ambiguity also includes not needing to feel as if one is in total control of everything all of the time, by trying to organize, schedule and plan everything out. It means not having to know all of the answers all of the time. So as a boss, a supervisor, a parent, or teacher, it would include a willingness and ability to say "I don't know" or "I'm not sure" sometimes.

Another aspect of tolerance for ambiguity is a willingness to accept that there are no guarantees in life. Many things we try in life involves a certain degree of risk, and when we take chances, things don't always work out. This requires accepting that life involves taking risks and having failures, and that nothing is foolproof or a sure thing.

Tolerance for ambiguity includes an acceptance of change as being a normal part of life, and that change is perhaps to only permanent thing in our rapidly progressing world.

A tolerance for ambiguity is a key factor in being able to deal with stress. The greater a person's tolerance, the better they're able to deal with the gray areas of life, the disorder, the doubt, the lack of guarantees, and change. This is a critical factor in maintaining successful personality and well-being.

11.   Sense Of Balance & Harmony

An eleventh aspect of successful personality is having a sense of balance and harmony. This is experienced in situations where a person is fully engaged in life, in total accord. Many people have this experience in their work, sports, relationships, art, and nature. A common example might be that of going to a theater to see a movie. As you go in the theater and sit down, you look at your watch and notice what time it is. The film starts and you find that the movie is very well done, it's totally engaging, it captivates you, and you become a part of the story. Some time later the film comes to an end and you come back to your senses and notice your watch and you observe that more than two hours have gone by, and you're not too sure just where you've been during that time. You may wonder what all has occurred out there in the world. For that period of time you've experienced a sense of unity, of harmony, you became a part of the film and the story. Time and space became rather irrelevant.

Many times people have this experience in communicating with another individual. You sit down and start talking and you have the feeling that you're on the same channel, the same wavelength, the same frequency. You express your self, putting your thoughts, ideas, and feelings into words, and the other person hears you, they understand you, and they respond back to you. You find that you're able to relate to them. You're able to understand what it is that they're expressing, and there's a sense of balanced closeness and intimate harmony.

A similar experience sometimes occurs with teams in sports, when the team is working together, there is a sense of balance and harmony, and oftentimes nothing the team does goes wrong, they're really hot, they're really on. When this occurs the team is often unbeatable, and they play exceptionally well.

The same process can occur on the job. This sense of balance and harmony involves a tuning-in process, a tuning in to some of the natural order and balances in one's environment. To be able to harmonize with one's world, with people, places and things, to be able to blend in, to become a part of it, to go with the flow, is a very satisfying, exciting and delightful experience.

It's somewhat paradoxical, however, in that we cannot force or control these experiences. We can't say for example, "Well, let's see, it's Tuesday, I think this afternoon at 4:00 p.m. I'll experience balance and harmony." The harder we try, the less likely it is to happen. We can be open to this experience, lay the ground work for it, and appreciate it when it occurs. Having this sense of balance and harmony is an important element of successful personality.

12.   Affirmative Life Attitudes

A twelfth element of successful personality is having affirmative life attitudes.   This involves a passionate investing of one's time and energy into the real world, into tasks to be completed, challenges to be met, and problems to be solved.   It includes having personal goals and directions in life which are positive, constructive, and life-enhancing. These can include such goals and directions as raising a family, developing a career, or investing your time and energies into causes and pursuits which matter to you.

Affirmative life attitudes include having a personal working philosophy of life, some guiding principles and values. The bottom line is a feeling that life is worthwhile, that it is worth the struggle.   It means having some personal reasons for getting up in the morning and carrying on with life.

To have a sense of meaning and purpose in life, to have a personal working philosophy, and a passion for living, are key elements in successful personality.

In Summary - Psyched to Succeed

It's important to keep in mind that no one person has all twelve elements of successful personality all of the time. Each individual has the potential and capacity for all twelve, and we all have them to varying degrees. We're also all lacking and deficient in different areas at different times in our lives.

It is useful to review these points, to increase our awareness and understanding of them, and to identify those areas where we may want to invest some additional time and effort. With this awareness and understanding of successful personality, we can nurture and develop more effective attitudes and behaviors.

When the elements of successful personality are coupled with hard work, discipline, and perseverance, the likelihood of succeeding in one's personal and professional endeavors is greatly enhanced.

On Real-Life Intelligence
The Edge For Successful Living

By "Dr. Dan" Matzke, PhD

FAQ's Addressed in this Program:

Why do I feel so alone and apart from things at times?
How can I cope with loneliness and separation in life?
Why is it so difficult to make
choices & commitments at times?
How can I effectively deal with freedom & responsibility?
Why do I feel so uncomfortable with changes at times?
How can I more effectively cope with endings in life?
Why do I feel like life is
meaningless and without purpose at times?
How can I find meaning & purpose in my life?
Why do I feel so much anxiety & tension at times?
How can I more effectively deal with stress in life?

Table Of Contents

Preface/Introduction:

This program explores what might best be called "Real-Life Intelligence". It goes beyond the basics of "emotional intelligence"… to the next level… which entails coming to terms with life & living. These are existential questions and concerns which humans have wrestled with throughout all of recorded history. Confronting these issues can be rather anxiety-provoking and disquieting, and it usually requires a relatively high level of emotional intelligence to even start the process. Ultimately, however, facing these matters can be very liberating and empowering, freeing a person to function more effectively, to thrive and to prosper.

What is "emotional intelligence"? Emotional intelligence refers to an awareness of and ability to manage emotions and create motivation. It is a set of personal and interpersonal skills (including the ability to apply knowledge & understanding) related to one's personality and behavior patterns, which results in a person being able to function more effectively in life.

What is "real-life intelligence"? Real-life intelligence refers to understanding and skills related to matters such as freedom & responsibility, choices & commitments, meaning & purpose, and changes & endings. Confronting and coming to terms with these ultimate concerns has very liberating and empowering benefits, greatly increasing one's ability to function effectively in personal and professional endeavors – far beyond that which is possible with just basic emotional intelligence.

Part 1 - On Aloneness & Separateness:

One basic life given, a psychological fact of life, is aloneness and separateness, the sense of being a part of, yet apart from. We enter into life alone, and we depart, or die alone. Anxiety, tension and conflict results from our awareness of our absolute aloneness, and we wish for contact, protection, and to be a part of a larger whole. No matter how close each of us becomes to another person, there remains a final unbridgeable gap, a separateness between us.

There are three forms of separateness and aloneness which are commonly experienced. One is interpersonal aloneness, a sense of loneliness or social separateness. This has been aggravated by the decline of several social aspects of our culture and lifestyle.

One is the decrease in family involvement. Oftentimes extended family members are several thousand miles apart, spread out and very separate. Church involvement has also gradually declined over the past few generations, reducing social contact. Neighborhoods have become more and more isolated. There is less of a neighborhood feeling and social interaction. These increases in interpersonal isolation over the past several generations have heightened the sense of personal aloneness.

A second type of isolation is intrapersonal - separations within. This often results from splits between our body, mind, and emotions. An example might be a split in which we do not trust our intuition or judgment - there is a split within ourselves. It can involve being out of touch with, or unaware of, one's own body. The mind may be moving alone at warp speed and not be aware of, honoring, or respecting some of the physical needs for nutrition or rest. Other splits might occur because of accepting as absolute, some of the "shoulds" and "oughts" that we were programmed with early in life, over one's own feelings, intuition, or preferences.

A third form of isolation can be referred to as worldly estrangement. This refers to a sense of a separation between one's self and the world, a feeling that you are not part of it all, that you do not fit. A phrase that captures it is that you are "in this world, but not of this world". There is a sense of strangeness. The film "E.T." captured this sense of not being at home, of being alien to the world.

To temper this sense of aloneness and separateness, we can use the world as a tool and absorb ourselves in the means available. Constructive ways through which we can deal with this sense of isolation can be found. One way of dealing with this condition is through creative activity. Creative activity results in a union of the artist with the material or product, a way of bridging the separateness. Another form of creative activity is sport, where a participant experiences a sense of union with the activity or apparatus. A gymnast, for example, can experience flowing movements that often result in a sense of oneness and harmony. The classic example of a Zen archer who is one with his bow and arrow, describes a means of dealing with the sense of separateness.

Another way in which we can deal with aloneness is through group membership, by joining social and professional groups, and by participating in their activities, customs and ceremonies. Participating in group activities helps to deal with feelings of aloneness and separateness. Through becoming part of a larger group or a larger system, we can temper isolation.

A third way of dealing with this basic given is through altered states of consciousness or awareness. Forms of altered states include meditation and prayer, through which a person can experience a sense of unity and oneness. Vigorous rhythmic exercise, such as running, bicycling and swimming, can also result in altered states of consciousness, in which the athlete experiences a sense of balance and harmony.

Perhaps one of the most satisfying ways of dealing with aloneness and separateness is through interpersonal union, or love, where two individuals become one in a relationship, experiencing a sense of closeness and intimacy. Sexual intimacy can result in a profound union including physical, mental and emotional elements. Relationships cannot eliminate isolation, yet aloneness can be shared. Love compensates for the pain of separateness. Relationships can provide a bridge from one alone self to another alone self.

There is however, a dilemma that we encounter in relationships, the dilemma of fusion versus isolation. Fusion... to leech or cling to - versus isolation... to be apart from and alone. This is a major developmental task for human beings; to relate to another person without reducing the other person to a tool, a defense against isolation and its resulting anxiety.

We need to accept the basic human condition of aloneness and separateness, and that it cannot be totally overcome. If not, we may seek desperately to avoid it, or to deny it. This can result in self-defeating and destructive behaviors. One form of self-defeating behavior that is a desperate attempt to overcome isolation is through developing dependent or manipulative relationships. This type of relationship, in which a person is desperately clinging to someone, clutching to them, trying to overcome the sense of aloneness, usually tends to alienate other people, driving them away, which in turn aggravates the aloneness and separateness the person felt originally.

Another extreme form of behavior which attempts to overcome separateness and isolation is fanatical immersion in causes and pursuits. This may include charity work, political causes or religious pursuits. Fanatical emersion often entails constant activity or excessive busyness. Workaholics who have a compulsive drivenness often reflect a desperate attempt to overcome a feeling of being separate, apart or alone.

Another destructive way of trying to avoid this given is through the use of drugs and alcohol, to obtain chemically induced sensations of oneness or harmony. A similar example of attempted escape can be through mysticism. Mysticism involves a sense of ego-loss through experiences of unity or cosmic oneness. This may result in a person "dropping out" of the world, shunning earthly obligations and responsibilities, and going on a relentless quest for mystical experiences in an attempt to overcome the feelings of aloneness and separateness.

Through facing and accepting aloneness and separateness as a given of human existence, we in effect reduce our anxiety and tension, and thereby are less likely to engage in self-defeating actions, in a desperate attempt to avoid or overcome this basic life condition.

Part 2 - On Choices & Commitments:

A second basic life given involves freedom and responsibility. Freedom refers to the absence of external structure, a lack of restrictions and limitations. Human beings have the literal freedom to author their own life design, their choices and commitments. This freedom results in anxiety from the realization that with freedom comes responsibility. If I have the freedom to choose what I shall do, then I am accountable for whatever I choose to do, or choose not to do. To deal with this awesome, anxiety-provoking condition, humans tend to seek structure, to seek out guidelines and rules of authority, as a way of shielding ourselves from absolute freedom. This is done in an attempt to avoid the reality that there are no universal imperatives in life; no absolute shoulds, oughts or musts.

Freedom presents us with the problem of choice. Since there is nothing that we have to do, and there are no absolute universal shoulds or oughts, the question then is "What do you want to do?"

Generally people are not ready for all this freedom. It results in a great deal of anxiety from the realization that one is truly accountable, and ultimately responsible for, one's own life. To avoid this reality a person may engage in a frantic search for someone or something to tell them what to do; to sacrifice one's freedom to avoid the anxiety of being responsible for one's own life. A person may choose to surrender their freedom to an institution, such as a legal or mental health institution, or a belief system, such as a religious dogma, or to another person through a dependent relationship. A person may seek to surrender their freedom, to avoid the responsibility of making choices and commitments.

Another way of shunning self-responsibility is to assume an "ultimate rescuer". This ultimate rescuer is generally viewed as a power that is outside of oneself, that adopts responsibility for us. This notion is often employed to quell anxiety, with the hope for some form of intervention to tell us how to live, or what choices to make. These forms of responsibility avoidance tend to impair a person's effectiveness, and to block mature functioning, which require the acceptance of self-responsibility.

Understanding freedom helps us to deal with responsibility assumption, which involves decision making, choices and commitments. A decision is a very lonely act. Decisions force us to accept personal responsibility, and confront us with anxiety through the realization that we are alone in the choice. It is our choice. A decision, and the resulting commitment, carries with it the connotation of finality. This is it... the impossibility of further possibility. That is the essence of what a decision involves - making a commitment that results in the impossibility of further possibility - the harsh reality that "alternatives exclude".

Many times in life we are faced with an A or B type choice, which can be very anxiety provoking. For then, we are committed to live with our choice, either A or B. As we travel down the road of life we encounter many "forks" in the road. We are repeatedly confronted with the alternatives of either taking the left or right path, with the resulting consequence of never knowing what "might have been" down the other road or choice. Alternatives do exclude. These basic conditions of life, the dilemma of freedom and responsibility, the reality that alternatives often exclude in choices and commitments, cannot be avoided or totally overcome. Through the acceptance of these givens, we can experience a liberating effect from the anxiety inherent in this human predicament, thereby reducing our use of defenses and self-limiting behaviors to deny or avoid these conflicts and dilemmas.

Part 3 - On Changes & Endings:

A third basic life given deals with changes and endings... the reality that everything fades. The experience of changes and endings in life is often very distressing. The myth of contemporary man is that he is finally in control, that through technology, nature itself can be tamed and made a servant of humanity. Changes and endings confront this myth, and teach us that the universe is vaster than our ability to control it, and more complex than our ability to totally explain it. Few people face or confront changes and endings freely or by choice. Usually life experiences confront us, and these may include changes and endings in relationships, jobs and careers, the loss of a loved one, or near death experiences through accidents or illnesses. If a person is willing to face changes and endings, including his own mortality, instead of avoiding or denying them, many valuable lessons can be learned. A confrontation with a change or ending often results in major shifts in attitudes and behaviors, and a person can make quantum leaps in their personal growth and development.

One of these areas of growth often involves a person's life perspectives and views. There is a realignment of life priorities, of what really matters, of what is important, and what is meaningful. Through facing changes and endings we learn that our unfinished business need not wait until we only have a few weeks, days, or hours to live. Life takes on a new sense of urgency. We do not have time to waste. We cannot really count on tomorrow. Through facing one's finiteness, a person can experience a sense of liberation from some of life's shoulds and oughts. Many of the social customs and rituals are not near as binding, or as restrictive as they once were. The incorporation of our transitoriness enriches life. It enables a person to extricate themselves from many of the smothering trivialities, to live more purposefully, more authentically, to be more open, honest, direct, and to assume more self-responsibility.

Through confronting changes and endings, many people experience an enhanced sense of living in the present... here and now... the idea that each moment can be counted as a gift, one day at a time, one moment at a time. There is much less dwelling on the past or wishful thinking for the future.

Another lesson that many people learn is that they have an increased appreciation and delight in some of the subtle beauties of life, including art, nature and people. Their senses seem to perk up. They tune into some of the subtlest little things. By being mindful of endings, one passes into a state of gratitude, of appreciation for the countless joys of existence.

Many people also experience deeper communication with loved ones, as a result of facing changes and endings. They start talking about things that matter, personal joys and concerns, hopes and dreams. There is a greater willingness to show caring and affection, more hugs, less small talk, less social chitchat and game playing. People start relating person-to-person, stepping out of their roles.

A somewhat paradoxical result of confronting this given is that many people find that they have fewer fears in life. There is a greater willingness to take risks, a desire to live a full life, measured not by the clock and quantity, but by quality, the quality of one's existence. People are not so much afraid of their death as they are afraid of the incompleteness of their life. A person who risks nothing does nothing, has nothing, and is nothing. He may avoid suffering, pain, may postpone death, but he limits his capacity to learn, to grow, and to live. By facing this life given, we find that we have fewer fears, and a greater willingness to take some of the risks that results in a fuller life.

Abraham Maslow, a leader in the field of psychology and education, wrote a letter to a friend after he had a major heart attack. In the letter he said, "The confrontation with death, and the reprieve from it, makes everything look so precious, so sacred, so beautiful, that I feel more strongly than ever the impulse to love it, to embrace it, and to let myself be overwhelmed by it. Death, and its ever-present possibility, makes love, passionate love, more possible. I wonder if we could love, if ecstasy would be possible at all, if we knew we would never die."

Through facing this basic given, each of us feels less futile, less helpless, and less alone, even when ironically what we come to understand is the fact that each of us is basically alone and helpless in the face of universal indifference. Uncertainty exists in life. There are no guarantees. Each of us needs to learn to co-exist with this uncertainty, to tolerate ambiguity, instead of frantically attempting to avoid or control these conditions. Dealing with changes and endings is a letting-go process. It is a skill that is needed and used throughout life. Through acceptance of change and ending as a part of life, including all the small mini-deaths that occur, there is a sense of peace and serenity. The saying "Everything Fades" summarizes it well. Being mindful of this given and surrendering to it gracefully can greatly enhance the joy and satisfaction one experiences in life. Acceptance helps to overcome the notion that changes and endings should be avoided, ought to be fair and just, or must be controlled.

Part 4 - On Life Meaning & Purpose:

A fourth basic life given relates to life meaning and purpose. We as human beings tend to be creatures in search for meaning and purpose, and our happiness and well-being is dependent on the extent to which we are able to experience a sense of meaning and purpose in life. Modern man's dilemma is that we are not told by instincts what we must do, or by waning traditions what we should, and oftentimes we do not know what it is that we want to do. The phenomenon of the "Sunday Neurosis" is a common occurrence, in which having free time makes many people aware of the fact that there is nothing that they want to do. Many people struggle with three day weekends. They can keep busy maybe Friday and Saturday, but come Sunday the question arises "What do I want to do with my free time?" When there is a distinct life vacuum, a lack of meaning, symptoms will rush in to fill it.

These symptoms often include obsessive/compulsive behaviors such as alcohol and drug abuse, or excessive work. The workaholic who says, "Gee, I have an extra day, I think I'll go into the office." It can include a variety of delinquent or illegal behaviors, or daredevilry - the taking of risks just for the rush of it, just to get some excitement. These are desperate attempts to fill the void, to overcome the sense of meaninglessness.

At this point in history many people have a lot of free time. Some work four day work weeks. Many have several weeks of vacation time, and oftentimes it is too much free time, in which a person is confronted with some disturbing questions. Free time is problematic because it confronts us with the question of what to do with our time. What is meaningful? What is satisfying? What should I do? What do I really want to do with my life? The issue of life meaning and purpose is one that human beings have wrestled with throughout all of recorded history. As human beings we have the capacity to be self-aware, to step outside of our self, to assume a detached view. This capacity for self-awareness and self-detachment can be very valuable and powerful. It also has some risks, however. There is a danger. There are some problems which occur when we step back too far, or when we stay there too long. When we assume a cosmic view or galactic perspective of life, we can get into trouble. This detached viewpoint tends to drain vitality from life. To assume it for a prolonged period of time can result in a sense of despair, and continued emersion in a detached viewpoint may be lethal. It can result in severe depression and suicidal thoughts. There is a saying that sums it up quite well: "Analysis leads to paralysis". If we are very busy analyzing life, asking all sorts of "why" or "what for" questions, we tend to get paralyzed. We are impaired. Our ability to engage in life, to fully participate, is blocked. The direct quest for the ultimate meaning of life can be a self-sabotaging endeavor.

The search for life meaning is paradoxical in that the more we search for it, the less we find it. A frantic search for the "goal" or "point" of life can lead to a sense of meaninglessness and despair - that nothing matters from a cosmic view or galactic perspective.

The answer, a sense of meaning and purpose in life, is found by looking away from the question, by disengaging from the cosmic viewpoint, and by engaging in life. Life is a gift. Take it, unwrap it, appreciate it, use it and enjoy it. Regardless of one's religious beliefs, philosophical views, or scientific approach to life, all humans are confronted with the same basic challenge of finding meaning and purpose in life. Although half-sure, we can wholeheartedly leap into engagement, immersing oneself in the stream of life… being fully present, here and now… getting into being human and the process of being.

There are three primary means to personal meaning and purpose. One is through creativity. Creativity in what we do, what we give to the world, in how we use our time and energy. This could include work, hobbies, sports, and service to others. Some examples might include art and teaching, caring relationships, or scientific discovery. To create or discover something new, to put something together in a different way, something of beauty, something of harmony. As for the question of "Why?" or "What for?" – For its own sake. It really needs no excuse or reason. Creativity is intrinsically rewarding and satisfying in and of itself. The creative process of using our time and energy results in joy and well-being. It is personally meaningful.

A second means to meaning is through experiences that we have - what we take in and what we get from the world. Through experiencing truth, beauty, the love of another human being, we experience a sense of meaning and purpose in life. Tuning into the natural order around us, tuning into the subtle and delicate balances in life, tuning into the harmony which exists, being aware of it, appreciating it, and delighting in it, results in a meaningful existence.

A third means to meaning centers on our attitude – our thinking and focus in life. Negative thinking tends to focus on "what is not" or "what cannot be", and results in a great deal of frustration and disappointment. In contrast, by focusing on "what is" and "what can be", life meaning and purpose looms. Meaning potentials and opportunities take form, and give us direction and purpose in life.

By not getting caught up in the thinking that one should or must have an answer to the question of "What's the ultimate meaning of life?", a person is freer to experience a sense of personal meaning and purpose in life, through passionate engagement, by doing and experiencing what is, and what can be.

Part 5 - On Anxiety, Tension & Stress:

A fifth basic life given is the stressful feeling of anxiety and tension, the sense of uncertainty, apprehension, uneasiness and pressure, which is a part of the human condition. It is an illusion to think that this condition can ever be completely overcome or avoided. With the human capacity for consciousness and awareness, comes the ability to see possibilities, many of which can be very distressing. These possibilities include not only the opportunity for success, joy, health, and happiness, but also the possibility or chance of failure, sadness, illness, and despair. This uniquely human capacity is a double edged sword, which requires a delicate balance to be used effectively. Each individual has a "comfort zone" of anxiety and tension, within which they can function. Too much or too little tension results in discomfort and impairment. It is a basic challenge in life to maintain this baseline of anxiety and tension within one's personally acceptable limits. For example with work, it is a challenge to maintain a level of demand and pace which is a balance between being bored and being overwhelmed. In physical and emotional endeavors, it is a challenge to maintain the delicate balance of "total control" versus "total chaos" or safety and security versus taking risks. It is a continual challenge to maintain the delicate balance between being totally engaged, and being detached, in the three arenas of life: love, work, and play.

Through engagement, we become immersed in the process of doing and experiencing life. Active involvement results in "losing oneself", including one's troubles and concerns. While this effectively reduces anxiety and tension, total, continual engagement results in the risk of getting lost, of being consumed, or going off on a tangent, which can be self-defeating and destructive.

Through detachment, a person can extricate themselves from the activities and busyness of life, and objectively observe the process with dispassionate regard. This perspective can result in a clear view of life's complexities, allowing an individual to guide and direct the course of their life. However, continued detachment results in an escalation of anxiety and tension, leading to a sense of apathy or despair, a feeling that nothing matters, or that it's all futile.

By balancing engagement and detachment, anxiety and tension can be maintained at an acceptable level. Through finding a personal balance in love, work and play, and striving to maintain this level within one's comfort zone, a person is better able to deal with anxiety and tension, which is a stressful life given.

In Summary

The five critical core issues reviewed often overlap and interact with each other, much like the strands of a rope. These are basic conflicts and dilemmas which all human beings struggle with:

1) No matter how close we get to another person, we still face life alone.

2) Each person has the ultimate responsibility for their choices and commitments, no matter how much guidance and advice they get from others.

---

3) Change is perhaps the only permanent thing in life, with many life changes and endings being unfair and unjust.

4) We can experience a sense of personal meaning and purpose in life, in spite of not having a definitive answer to the question "What is the ultimate meaning of life?"

5) Anxiety and tension is a normal part of life, which cannot be totally overcome, only kept in balance.

There are no "fixes", so to speak, no way to do away with these anxiety-provoking conditions of life. Through confrontation and acceptance of how it is, we can experience liberation from the frantic and desperate attempt to avoid or overcome these givens, and from the thinking that things should be, ought to be, or must be, different, for us to be happy. Through acceptance, we can experience a sense of peace and serenity, which frees us to live life more fully and richly, in more effective and successful ways.

Addendum

"Wings Of Wisdom"

Uplifting Essence Essays

By Psychologist

"Dr. Dan" Matzke, PhD

On Personal Effectiveness
Seven Powerful Pointers

On Life & Living
Seven Golden Guidelines

On The Art & Technique Of
Mindfulness

On Personal Effectiveness
Seven Powerful Pointers

By Psychologist "Dr. Dan" Matzke, PhD

Planning
Think ahead - be proactive.
Prioritize and organize future actions.

Preparedness
Aim for anticipation and prevention.
Strive to be ready for future needs.

Pacing
Aspire for flow without force.
Adjust the pace to fit the place.

Persistence
Endeavor for progress and progression.
Take the steps one at a time.

Perspective
For best perspective - be objective.
Seek to see the big picture.

Patience
Be here – now.
Question the need to hurry or rush.

Personal-Responsibility
Focus on choices and commitments.
Get real… Get a grip… Get on with it.

Author's Note: While the above pointers are basic and primary, they are critical and essential for personal effectiveness. The guideposts can also point to matters that one is ignoring or avoiding (due to fear, dread, etc.) which are road blocks and barriers towards the next step and/or the next level in one's endeavors and life journey. A good "rule of thumb" is that ten percent (10%) extra effort invested in using these principles results in a ninety percent (90%) difference. Developing one's awareness of and practicing these pointers and self-coaching tools can yield significant benefits – enabling one to "take a hold of life" and face challenges with courage and confidence. Other publications by Dr. Dan are available at *DrDanMatzkePhD.com* PS – You are invited to share this essay.

On Life & Living
Seven Golden Guidelines

By Psychologist "Dr. Dan" Matzke, PhD

Truth
Seek truth, truthfulness and genuineness.
Be real, honest and sincere,
And seek others who are authentic.

Beauty
Look for beauty and good in nature, art and people.
Appreciate aesthetic magnificence and grandeur.

Excellence
Strive for excellence and quality in all endeavors.
Enjoy the elements of grace and elegance.

Wisdom
Seek wisdom and the prudent use of knowledge.
Aim to use good reasoning and judgment.

Justice
Strive for justice, fairness and reasonableness.
Be compassionate and caring with integrity.

Courage
Have the courage to take a stand for that which is best.
Be courageous with valor and gallantry.

Moderation
Seek balance and harmony in life.
Exercise moderation and temperance in living.

Author's Note: The above thoughts, ideas and perspectives are drawn from great seminal thinkers throughout all of recorded history. These are wise time-tested principles which can be powerful tools - useful in guiding one's daily actions toward life success and happiness. Interested readers are referred to classical writings in literature, philosophy and spirituality for further study.   Other publications by Dr. Dan are available at *DrDanMatzkePhD.com* PS – You are invited to share this essay.

On The Art & Technique Of

Mindfulness

Powerful Principles & Practices

For Personal Development,
Peak Performance & Well-Being

By Psychologist "Dr. Dan" Matzke, PhD

This essence essay considers the art and technique of mindfulness – which can be described as a mental state of clear minded awareness that is unencumbered, unfettered and unhurried. The art of mindfulness entails being fully present to experience and savor being alive, awake and aware. The technique of mindfulness involves consciously focusing one's attention on thoughts, feelings and actions, many of which can at times be self-defeating and toxic. Three core issues can be identified which often overlap and interact with each other, much like the strands of a rope. These are natural tendencies and habit patterns which all human beings struggle with:

Keep Critical, Judgmental & Negative Thinking
In Check

Nurture
Positive Perspectives

Temper Unfounded Fears & Self-Doubts

Develop A
Trusting Attitude

Be Cautious Of Consumption
By The Past & The Future

Practice Being Present
Here & Now

Author's Note:

The above principles of mindfulness are time-tested realistic practices, which were first articulated over 2500 years ago. These ideas are powerful pointers and skills which can greatly enhance personal effectiveness and well-being. Other programs and books by Dr. Dan are available at *DrDanMatzkePhD.com* PS - You are invited to share this essay.